Lerner *SPORTS*

SPORTS
VIPs

MEET
T. J. WATT

ELLIOTT SMITH

Lerner Publications ◆ Minneapolis

SPORTS THRILLS *MEET* RESEARCH SKILLS

Lerner SPORTS

Free Database Trial: **lernersports.com**

Lerner Publications Company
An imprint of Lerner Publishing Group, Inc.
241 First Avenue North
Minneapolis, MN 55401 USA

For reading levels and more information, look up this title at www.lernerbooks.com.

Main body text set in Aptifer Slab LT Pro. Typeface provided by Linotype AG.

Editor: Matt Doeden
Lerner team: Sue Marquis

Library of Congress Cataloging-in-Publication Data

Names: Smith, Elliott, 1976– author.
Title: Meet T. J. Watt : Pittsburgh Steelers superstar / Elliott Smith.
Description: Minneapolis, MN : Lerner Publications, [2024] | Series: Sports VIPs | Includes bibliographical references. | Audience: Ages 7–11 | Audience: Grades 4–6 | Summary: "Pittsburgh Steelers linebacker T. J. Watt learned to chase down quarterbacks at the University of Wisconsin. In 2021, he led the NFL in sacks and won the Defensive Player of the Year award"— Provided by publisher.
Identifiers: LCCN 2022055312 (print) | LCCN 2022055313 (ebook) | ISBN 9781728490953 (library binding) | ISBN 9798765603987 (paperback) | ISBN 9798765601358 (ebook)
Subjects: LCSH: Watt, T. J., 1994– —Juvenile literature. | Pittsburgh Steelers (Football team)—Juvenile literature. | Football players—United States—Biography—Juvenile literature. | BISAC: JUVENILE NONFICTION / Biography & Autobiography / Sports & Recreation
Classification: LCC GV939.W3624 S65 2024 (print) | LCC GV939.W3624 (ebook) | DDC 796.332092 [B]—dc23/eng/20230103

LC record available at https://lccn.loc.gov/2022055312
LC ebook record available at https://lccn.loc.gov/2022055313

Manufactured in the United States of America
1-53026-51044-2/28/2023

TABLE OF CONTENTS

>>>>>>>>>>>>>>>>>

RECORD DAY

It was cold and rainy in Baltimore, Maryland. But T. J. Watt was red hot. Watt and the Pittsburgh Steelers were playing the Baltimore Ravens on January 9, 2022. It was the last game of the regular season. The Steelers linebacker was all over the field.

The Steelers needed a win to make the playoffs. And Watt had a chance at making history. All season, he had used his speed and strength to bring down opposing quarterbacks. He entered the game with 21.5 sacks. He needed just one more to tie the NFL record for most sacks in a season.

FAST FACTS

DATE OF BIRTH: October 11, 1994

POSITION: linebacker

LEAGUE: National Football League (NFL)

PROFESSIONAL HIGHLIGHTS: was the NFL Defensive Player of the Year in 2021; holds the record for most sacks in one season with 22.5; is the highest-paid defensive player in the NFL

PERSONAL HIGHLIGHTS: grew up in Pewaukee, Wisconsin; his brothers, J. J. and Derek Watt, also play in the NFL; is married to former soccer player Dani Rhodes

Watt (*number 90*) chases down quarterback Tyler Huntley (*number 2*) in the final game of the 2021 season.

In the second quarter, the Steelers led 3–0. The Ravens were deep in Pittsburgh territory. Baltimore quarterback Tyler Huntley took the snap. The Steelers defense quickly closed in around him. Watt spun past one Ravens player. He ducked under another. Watt reached out and dragged Huntley to the ground for a sack.

Watt's teammates raised their arms in celebration. Watt delivered his famous sack dance, kicking his leg high into the air. He had just tied Pro Football Hall of Famer Michael Strahan for the most sacks in one season. The record had stood for more than 20 years.

Thanks to Watt's efforts, the Steelers won the game and made the playoffs. Watt became the NFL's Defensive Player of the Year. He is one of the most feared linebackers in the NFL. And he's only getting better.

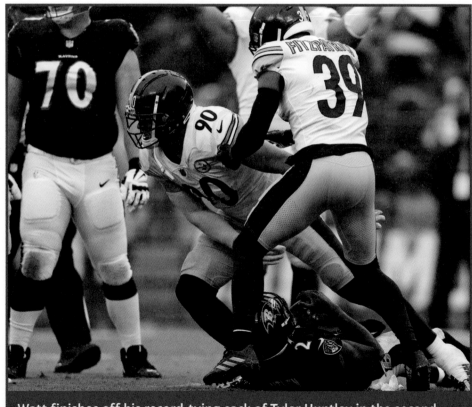

Watt finishes off his record-tying sack of Tyler Huntley in the second quarter of Pittsburgh's win over the Ravens.

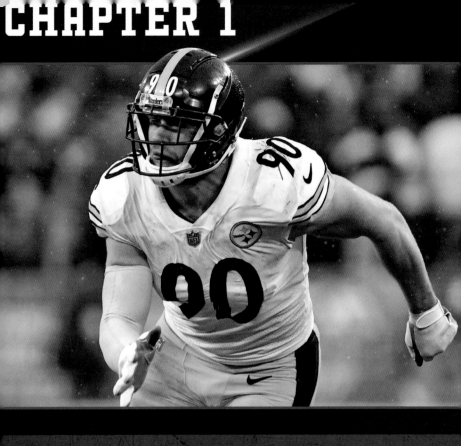

CHAPTER 1

FOOTBALL FAMILY

That Watt wound up playing football is no surprise. He was almost born into the sport. Trent Jordan Watt was born October 11, 1994, in Pewaukee, Wisconsin. His father was a firefighter. His mother was vice president of a company that made sure buildings are safe.

T. J. was the youngest of three boys. His brothers, J. J. and Derek, started playing football early. T. J. soon joined them in neighborhood games.

"For football we connected three neighbor backyards to make one huge football field," T. J. said. "We prided ourselves on being competitive. J. J. is five years older than me and Derek is two years older, but they always included me in everything they did."

The village of Pewaukee lies along Pewaukee Lake in eastern Wisconsin.

T. J. grew up playing a lot of sports. Football was his best sport. It was a natural fit. J. J. was a star at Pewaukee High School, and Derek soon followed. By the time T. J. arrived, the Watt name was legendary.

Watt looked up to his brother J. J. (*center*), who starred for the Wisconsin Badgers.

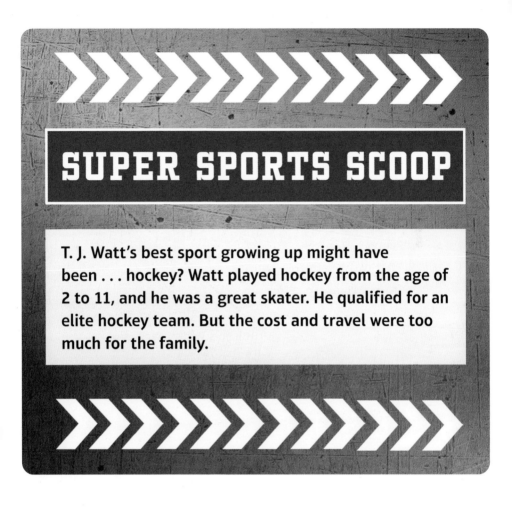

T. J. Watt's best sport growing up might have been . . . hockey? Watt played hockey from the age of 2 to 11, and he was a great skater. He qualified for an elite hockey team. But the cost and travel were too much for the family.

Like his brothers, T. J. was very successful as a high school football player. At Pewaukee, he played several positions. He was a tight end, quarterback, linebacker, and punter. In his junior year, T. J. had 27 catches for 505 yards. As a senior, he moved to quarterback. T. J. led Pewaukee to an undefeated regular season before losing in the playoffs. And he continued to grow.

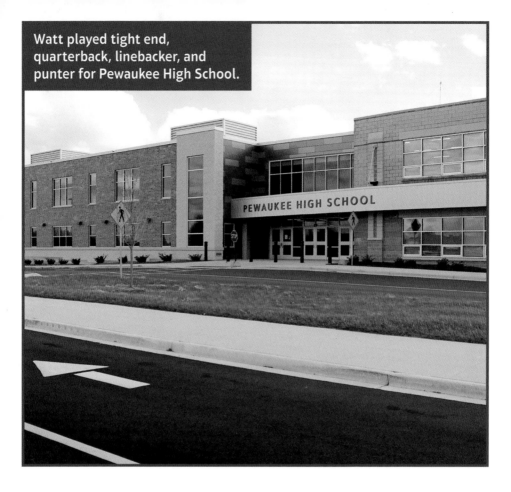

Watt played tight end, quarterback, linebacker, and punter for Pewaukee High School.

T. J. was a rising prospect. Several colleges wanted him. He visited Northern Illinois University. He considered the University of Minnesota. But the decision was easy. T. J. chose to follow his brothers and accept a scholarship to the University of Wisconsin. The Badgers wanted him to play tight end.

T. J. was ready for the next step in his football journey. But it would not be a straight or smooth path to glory.

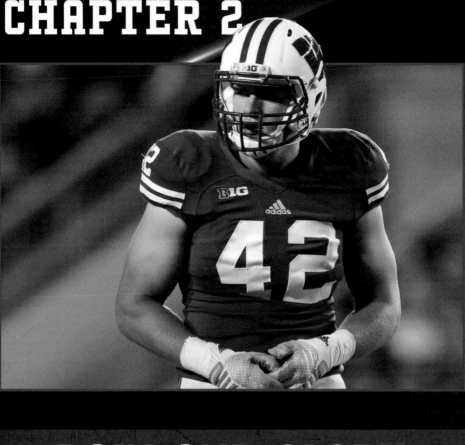

CHAPTER 2

PAIN AND GLORY

In 2013, Watt arrived on the University of Wisconsin campus. He was not quite ready for the demands of college football. The team decided he needed a redshirt year. That meant he could practice with the team but not play in games. It would give him time to get stronger.

Late in the 2014 season, Watt was blocking in practice. He injured his right knee. It was a painful injury with a long recovery. Then, in 2015, he hurt his knee again. For a second time, he needed surgery—and he still hadn't played a college game. Watt considered quitting football. He decided to stick with the game. It meant too much to him to walk away.

"There are so many people that don't love to practice, but when the game is taken away from you, you'll give anything to just be out there on the practice field," Watt said. "That's something I carry with me today."

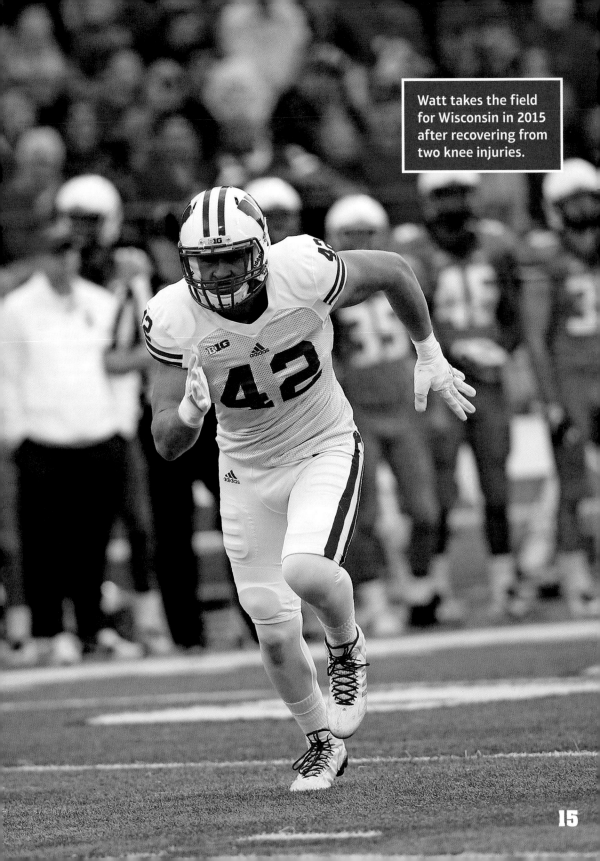

Watt takes the field for Wisconsin in 2015 after recovering from two knee injuries.

The coaches at Wisconsin presented Watt with an idea. Would he like to switch to linebacker? A different position might be easier on his knees. Watt agreed to the change. He didn't play in every game in 2015, as a sophomore. He made only seven tackles.

SUPER SPORTS SCOOP

Watt earned many honors during his junior season. He was selected to the All-Big Ten first team. He was named second-team All-American by the Associated Press. These teams included some of the best college football players in the country.

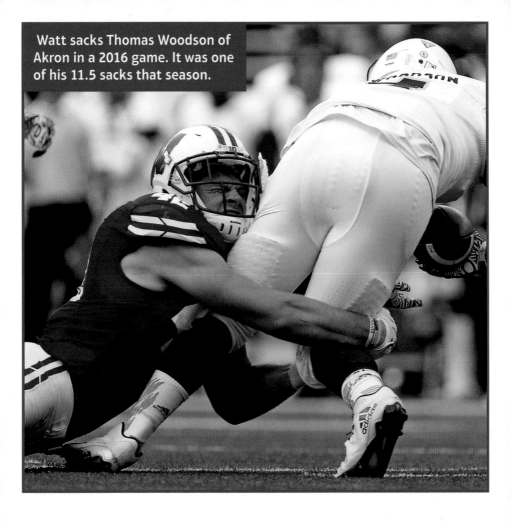

Watt sacks Thomas Woodson of Akron in a 2016 game. It was one of his 11.5 sacks that season.

Watt was ready to make an impact as a junior. He spent the off-season training. He was big at 6 feet 4 (1.9 m) and 240 pounds (109 kg). Watt used his size and speed to sack quarterbacks all season. In 14 games, he recorded 11.5 sacks and 63 tackles. The Badgers won 11 games and finished as the ninth-ranked team in college football. Watt became an All-American for his great play.

CHAPTER 3

SACK MASTER

Watt had a lot to prove before entering the NFL. He had only played one full season of college football. The NFL Scouting Combine was an important step. There, college players perform drills in front of NFL coaches and scouts.

Watt impressed a lot of scouts with his performance. Watt showed the scouts that he had the mix of speed, strength, and agility to succeed in the NFL. Yet some teams weren't sure about him. His injury history worried them. Many experts did not think he would go in the first round of the draft.

Watt answers questions during the 2017 NFL Scouting Combine.

Watt poses with Steelers president Art Rooney II after Pittsburgh selected him in the 2017 NFL Draft.

The Pittsburgh Steelers have a long history of defensive excellence. Fans called their 1970s defenses the Steel Curtain. Since then, the Steelers have built teams on tough defense. That made Watt a perfect fit.

On April 27, 2017, the Steelers selected Watt with the 30th pick in the first round of the NFL Draft. Some people were surprised he was selected that high. But Watt's NFL dreams had become reality. The Steelers put Watt in their starting lineup right away. He quickly proved that he belonged. In his first NFL game, Watt had two sacks and intercepted a pass.

Watt's ability to blitz the quarterback made him special. In his next two seasons, Watt reached double digits in sacks. After the 2019 season, Watt's teammates named him Pittsburgh's Most Valuable Player. He also played in his first Pro Bowl, the NFL's all-star game. He played on the same team as his brother J. J. Watt.

Watt made an immediate impact for the Steelers during his rookie season.

Watt's first few years in the NFL could not have gone any better. But he wasn't satisfied. He still had a few goals. "To be able to be recognized as the best defensive player of the year is definitely something I strive for," he said.

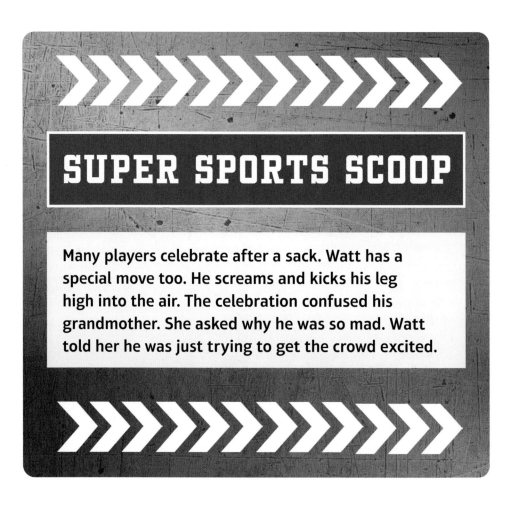

SUPER SPORTS SCOOP

Many players celebrate after a sack. Watt has a special move too. He screams and kicks his leg high into the air. The celebration confused his grandmother. She asked why he was so mad. Watt told her he was just trying to get the crowd excited.

CHAPTER 4

BEST OF THE BEST

Before the start of the 2020 season, Watt got a nice surprise. The Steelers added his brother Derek to the team. With his brother playing offense, Watt put together an amazing season on defense. He led the NFL in sacks with 15. He also led the league in tackles for loss and quarterback hits.

T. J. (*right*) talks with his brother Derek during a game in 2022.

Watt made a case to become Defensive Player of the Year. But Watt finished second to Aaron Donald of the Los Angeles Rams. Watt said he was not disappointed.

The Steelers rewarded Watt's excellence with a new contract. In 2021, he signed a four-year contract for $112 million. That made him the NFL's highest-paid defensive player. His teammates were thrilled. "He's the best in the world at what he does," Steelers linebacker Alex Highsmith said.

Watt raised the bar again in the 2021 season. Not only did he tie the NFL sack record, but he led the league in several other stats. He did this despite missing a game to injury. In February 2022, Watt won the NFL Defensive Player of the Year award. His fellow players voted him the sixth-best player in the league.

Watt drags down quarterback Justin Fields during a 2021 game against the Chicago Bears.

Watt started 2022 strong. In the first game, he got a sack and made six tackles in Pittsburgh's win over the Cincinnati Bengals. But he suffered an injury late in the game that forced him to miss two months. The Steelers struggled without him, going 1–6 while he was out. The team missed the playoffs.

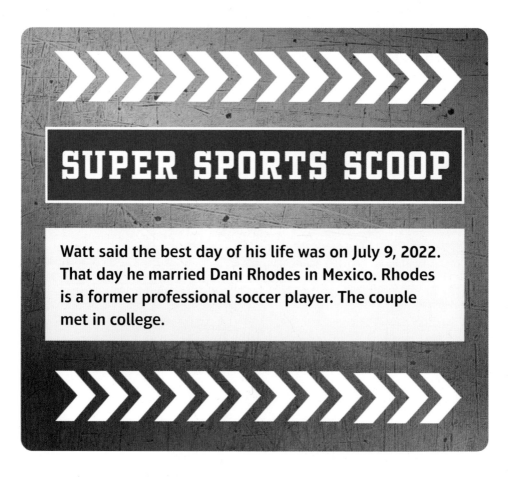

SUPER SPORTS SCOOP

Watt said the best day of his life was on July 9, 2022. That day he married Dani Rhodes in Mexico. Rhodes is a former professional soccer player. The couple met in college.

Quarterback Sam Darnold protects the ball as Watt pulls him to the ground in a 2022 game.

Despite his success, Watt continues to work hard. He is focused on leading the Steelers to a Super Bowl victory. And he wants the opportunity to write his name again in the NFL record books.

"I am definitely not satisfied," he said. "I am trying to continue to grow and be one of the best who ever played this game."

T. J. WATT
CAREER STATS

GAMES PLAYED:

87

TACKLES:

333

TACKLES FOR LOSS:

88

SACKS:

77.5

INTERCEPTIONS:

6

FORCED FUMBLES:

23

Stats are accurate through the 2022 NFL season.

GLOSSARY

agility: the ability to move quickly and easily

blitz: when linebackers or backs rush the quarterback

combine: an event where prospects undergo tests and drills for NFL teams

draft: when teams take turns choosing new players

prospect: a player who is likely to succeed at a higher level of play

redshirt: a year when a college football player can't play in games but can practice

sack: when a defender tackles the quarterback for a loss of yards

scholarship: money given to a student to help pay for their education

scout: a person who studies players for a football team

snap: putting the football in play by quickly passing it between the legs to a teammate

SOURCE NOTES

9 Douglas Clark, "Steelers All-Pro T.J. Watt Talks Pewaukee High School Football ahead of the National USA TODAY High School Sports Awards Show," *USA Today*, July 23, 2021, https://www.usatoday.com/story/sports/highschool/sports-awards/2021/07/23/steelers-linebacker-t-j-watt-talks-usa-today-high-school-sports-awards/8063457002/.

14 Clark.

22 Myles Simmons, "T. J. Watt: I'm Not Huge on Individual Goals but I Was Striving for DPOY," ProFootballTalk, February 11, 2022, https://profootballtalk.nbcsports.com/2022/02/11/t-j-watt-im-not-huge-on-individual-goals-but-i-was-striving-for-dpoy/.

24 Brooke Pryor, "How Will the Pittsburgh Steelers Regroup after T. J. Watt Injury?," *ESPN*, September 13, 2022, https://www.espn.com/nfl/story/_/id/34578471/how-pittsburgh-steelers-regroup-tj-watt-injury.

27 Mark Kaboly, "T. J. Watt Definitely Not Satisfied after Historic Season," Athletic, May 24, 2022, https://theathletic.com/3331407/2022/05/24/tj-watt-steelers-otas/.

LEARN MORE

Goodman, Michael E. *Pittsburgh Steelers*. Mankato, MN: Creative Education, 2023.

Hill, Christina. *Aaron Donald*. Minneapolis: Lerner Publications, 2022.

Lowe, Alexander. *G.O.A.T. Football Linebackers*. Minneapolis: Lerner Publications, 2023.

National Football League
https://NFL.com

Sports Illustrated Kids: Football
https://sikids.com/football

T. J. Watt
https://www.steelers.com/team/players-roster/t-j-watt/

INDEX

PHOTO ACKNOWLEDGMENTS

Image credits: AP Photo/Tom DiPace, p. 4; Karl Merton Ferron/The Baltimore Sun/Tribune News Service/Getty Images, p. 6; Patrick Smith/ Getty Images, p. 7; Randy Litzinger/Icon Sportswire/Getty Images, p. 8; Tony Savino/Shutterstock, p. 9; AP Photo/Cal Sport Media, pp. 10, 18; Courtesy of Pewaukee High School, p. 12; AP Photo/John Fisher/Cal Sport Media, p. 13; AP Photo/Scott Boehm, pp. 15, 24; Dylan Buell/Getty Images, p. 17; Robin Alam/Icon Sportswire/Getty Images, p. 19; AP Photo/ Keith Srakocic, p. 20; Al Pereira/Getty Images, p. 21; Eakin Howard/Getty Images, pp. 23, 27; Emilee Chinn/Getty Images, p. 25. Design elements: The Hornbills Studio/Shutterstock; Tamjaii9/Shutterstock.

Cover: Cal Sport Media via AP Images.